CONTENTS

1st Edition
Compiled and edited by Richard Blacklaw-Jones.
Printed by T J International, Cornwall.
Published by Pembrokeshire Prospectors 1997.

ISBN No 0-9532137-0-6

Acknowledgments

The Pembrokeshire Prospectors could not have produced this book in the first place without the financial support of Haverfordwest Town Council and we take great pleasure in thanking them publicly in this book. Other individuals and companies also helped us financially and we list them opposite.

We would like to thank all the members of the club who helped in the production of the book, some by giving us access to finds, some by spending hours at a word processor. In particular thanks should go to Adrian Young for his excellent illustrations and James Giles for his photography, to Terrene Smith for fund-raising, and to all three for their help with individual chapters. Others who helped with production of chapters are Jack Tree our Treasurer and Trevor Davies, Vice-Chairman. We need also to thank various persons for their specialist help. In no particular order we thank Mr Tom Lloyd for his help with local family crests, Mr Dillwyn Miles FSA for his Heraldic knowledge and advice. We need to thank Mr Mark Redknap and Mr Edward Besley both the of National Museum of Wales who have helped us identify so many of our finds. Special thanks should go to Dilys and Stephen Penney of Far West Design who have been invaluable with their help and advice as to the nuts and bolts of this book's production. Rachel Maclean-Walker for her patience with seemingly endless amendments and last minute typing. Lastly we need to thank our various landowners who let us detect upon their land. Without them we would not have found many of the artefacts seen in this book and we hope they are as proud of seeing them published as we, the finders are.

If we have forgotten to thank anyone or to credit anyone properly anywhere in this book the fault lies with myself. My position as Chairman is where the buck stops and speaking personally if I may for a moment, my role has privileged me to meet all sorts of interesting people in the past few years and also to be part of the production team for this book. It has been hard work, but I've enjoyed it and now I hope you the reader will enjoy it too and perhaps be stimulated to try our hobby of metal detecting

HAVERFORDWEST TOWN COUNCIL

Dilwyn Miles, FSA.

Butterhill Farms,
St. Ishmaels.

GREENS
M O T O R
H O L D I N G S
L I M I T E D

 Cory
Towage

"THE BEST IN THE WEST"
**SEWING & KNITTING
MACHINE CENTRE
Haverfordwest**

John Roche, Solicitor,
Brighton Chambers,
Pembroke

Pembrokeshire
Stan rosenthal: Artist in Residence
Saint Davids

Baring Gould Lodge
9272
Snowdrop Lane
Haverfordwest

PEMBROKESHIRE PROSPECTORS
A BRIEF HISTORY

In 1977 a group of metal detecting enthusiasts got together to organise a club for their hobby and to encourage interest in Pembrokeshire's history. The first meetings were held at (the old) Castle Museum in Haverfordwest and, although the venue has changed, meetings are still held on the first Thursday of the month.

During the first ten years the club had a bottle collecting section. These were a group of members who researched the locations of old (mostly Victorian) rubbish dumps and having gained permission, dug out a slice of history, not only with old beer and pop bottles from local manufacturers, but decorative pot lids, clay pipes and other discarded items from a past age. Sadly as these old tips were covered and in some cases built on, so the opportunities to recover items dwindled and ceased.

The Pembrokeshire Prospectors are a fixture at many of the local agricultural and vintage shows and members give their time freely in order to exhibit their finds to the public at these shows or any other venue offered. This promotes our hobby and shares our knowledge with the people of Pembrokeshire. Many of the artefacts or coins discovered have been donated to museums both local and national. This is in keeping with our aim of promoting interest in local history and of promoting our hobby. To further these aims the society has members who are available to give lectures to any interested group.

Part of the attraction of our hobby is that our finds often contribute to local historical knowledge and in some cases help to make clear previously mysterious periods of times. For example, in recent years the Society has established evidence that the Roman presence in, and influence upon Pembrokeshire was greater than previously believed. The Society members have also discovered and recorded a previously unknown medieval fair or market ground on the site of the new St Davids link road into Haverfordwest.

Most recently a society member recovered the largest Civil War coin hoard even found in Wales (see inside for further details).
The society's members regularly assist archaeologists on excavations in and around Pembrokeshire.This exercise has been particularly interesting as both

parties have learnt that we can be of mutual assistance.

Over the years the society's members have removed tonnes of metallic rubbish from the various places searched. Beaches have been cleaned of the nuisance ring pulls and the accumulated scrap metals have benefited charitable organisations.

Lastly the society offers a free service to anyone who has lost something metallic.This could be a vital piece of farm machinery or a sentimentally valuable piece of jewellry.

The Pembrokeshire Prospectors Society now meets at The RAOB Club, Snowdrop Lane, Haverfordwest on the first Thursday of the month at 7.30pm. New members are always welcome and we currently have a membership of around thirty from all walks of life.

James Giles,
Secretary.

Bronze Age Pembrokeshire

Metal first appeared in use in Britain around 2000BC. The people who were settled in Pembrokeshire at around this time left evidence of their occupation at known sites Rhoscrowther, Castlemartin and Talbenny. These are burial sites called cairns or barrows. Very little other evidence such as artifacts have been found in Pembrokeshire. It is significant that members of the Pembrokeshire Prospectors have made several finds of Bronze Age artifacts including an example of the earliest metal technology in Britain. These finds have been made away from the known sites of Bronze Age occupation.

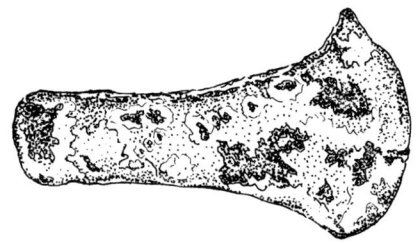

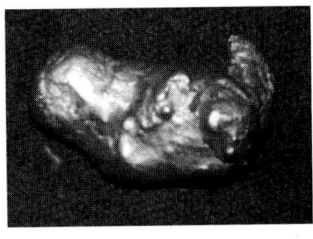

Given Pembrokeshire's nearness to Ireland, it has long been thought that there was trade during Bronze Age times between Ireland and Pembrokeshire. A metal detecting find from a North Pembrokeshire beach appears to support this theory. This gold nugget weighs 22.68g and when compared with Irish Bronze Age gold metalwork shows the same kind of impurities as found in them. It is reasonable to suppose that this nugget is of Irish gold and was brought to Pembrokeshire by an Irish goldsmith only to be lost on the beach. Imagine his annoyance and frustration!?!!?? Other Bronze Age finds have been made at this same beach in North Pembrokeshire and help to support the idea of a trade route to and from Ireland passing through this beach and Pembrokeshire. These finds include the copper flat Celt axe illustrated above and a Bronze Palstave axe dating to 1250BC (see illustration overleaf).

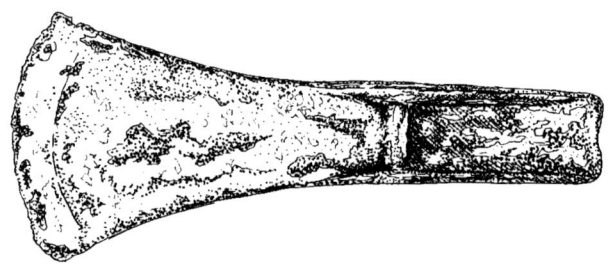

North Pembs Beach Palstave Axe 1250BC

Other beaches in Pembrokeshire seem to hold Bronze Age relics. Occasionally, a drowned landscape is revealed by storms which shift huge quantities of sand and shingle to reveal a landscape of flattened trees and peat. This is the drowned land which figures in the Welsh Folk tales of Seisennyn or Seisyllt the Drunkard and Cantre'r Gwaelod or The Lower Hundred. This landscape has revealed several Bronze Age finds illustrated below.

Again after storms had shifted several feet of sand and shingle the drowned

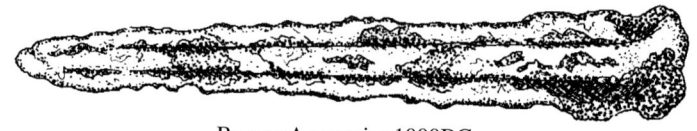

Bronze Age rapier 1000BC

landscape was revealed. It now consists of deep peat deposits and lots of tree trunks some still with roots into the peat, some over on their side. In the peat was discovered the Bronze Age rapier illustrated above. This one is particularly rare because it is made to be about six inches (15.5 cms) long. On the same day at the same beach a Bronze Age spearhead was found by a different detectorist.

This spear head was designed to fit onto a long shaft and would have been tied into place via the loops (which have not survived on this example). As to its use, it was most probably a weapon of war but its find location, deep in the peat under Newgale beach would probably indicate a hunting situation when it was lost. Probably it was aimed at a wild boar, the Twrch Trwyth of the Mabinogi even? Whatever ... it seems to have missed its target and been lost to the thrower as well, or perhaps the boar got him!

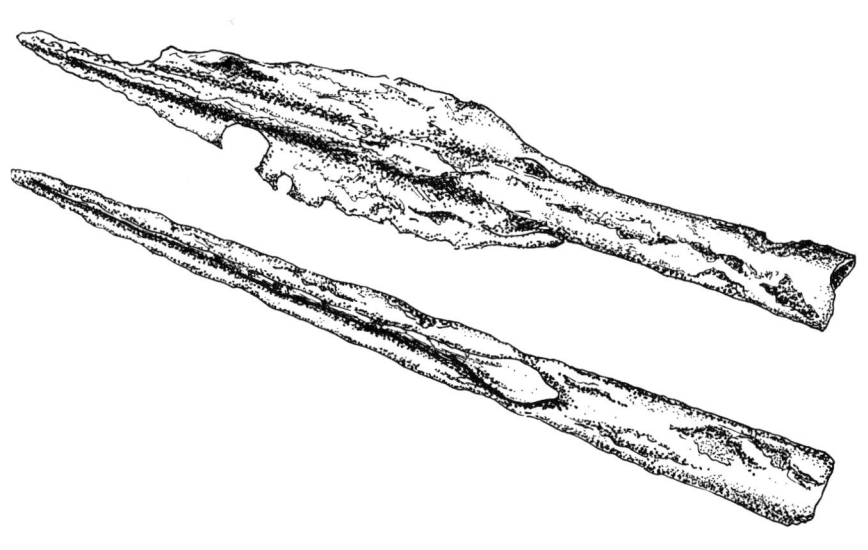

Basal Looped, leaf shaped, socketed Bronze Spearhead. Middle Bronze Age Type. 1200 - 1000 BC

Beaches have been kind the the Prospectors especially with Bronze Age finds. Another beach in South Pembrokeshire had been "scoured off" by the tide and the storms and a lucky detectorist was there in time to find a Late Bronze Age hoard as pictured below. The hoard contained three socketed axes, two broken bronze blades and twenty two bronze ingots. These ingots appear to have originated in South West England. Perhaps the owner had only just arrived in Wales by sea when he had to bury these artifacts or perhaps he was waiting for the boat to come in. His loss was our gain for this hoard was described as "of the first importance" by the National Museum of Wales.

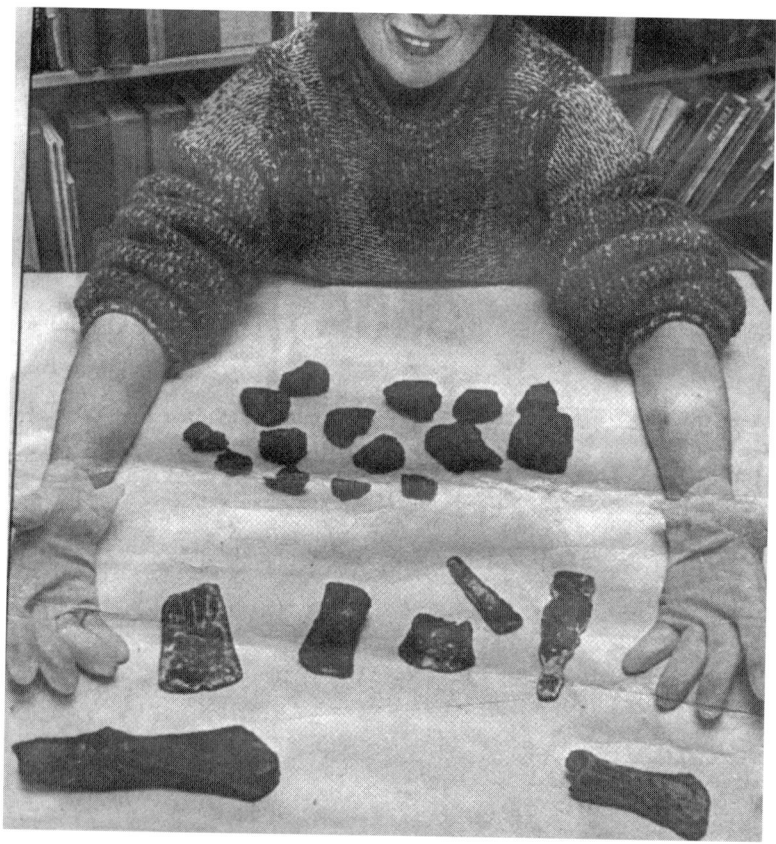

Western Telegraph

This broken section of a socketed axe-head dates to 900-700BC and was found in the same field as the terret ring in the Iron Age chapter (next). This field is close to the River Cleddau, and one wonders whether there was a crossing point nearby. There is no evidence of any settlement nearby to explain the presence of these artefacts.

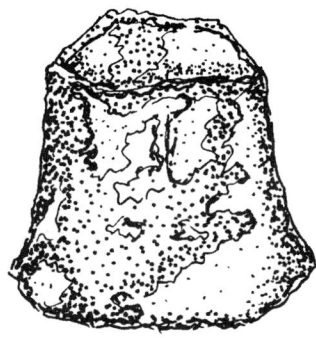

The socketed axe was a technological step forward for Bronze Age smiths. Being hollow saved on metal, which was obviously hard to come by at this time. Being hollow also meant that a shaped piece of wood could fit into it (see illustration). This arrangement gave better shock absorbency and meant that the axe-head stayed on the shaft better.

Earlier forms of axe-heads needed complicated lashing onto their shafts or necessitated splitting the shaft to fit the axe head onto it. These earlier designs have been tested by archaeologists and have proven less serviceable than the socketed design.

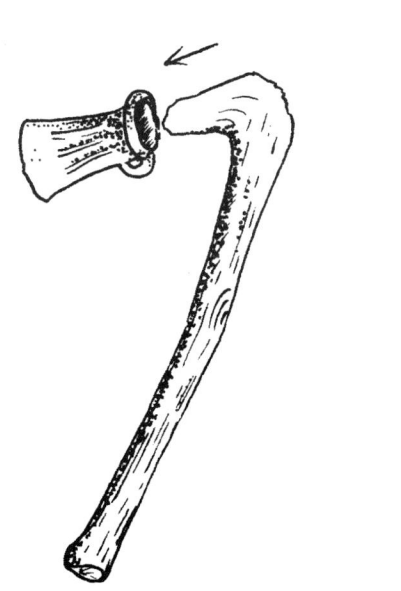
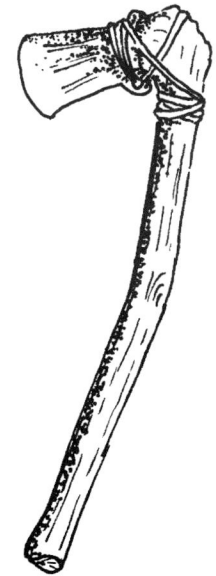

Iron Age Pembrokeshire 600BC - 45BC

Very little has been found of the Iron Age in Pembrokeshire. There are numerous Iron Age occupation camps, etc. known in Pembrokeshire but the finds rate of the Prospectors has not been great. What has been found is illustrated below.

This next item is also fragmentary. It is the remains of a terret ring or rein guide from a chariot of the Iron Age, circa. 100BC.

This would have been used to orient the harness straps from horses and helped prevent them tangling and thus making the chariot unguidable.

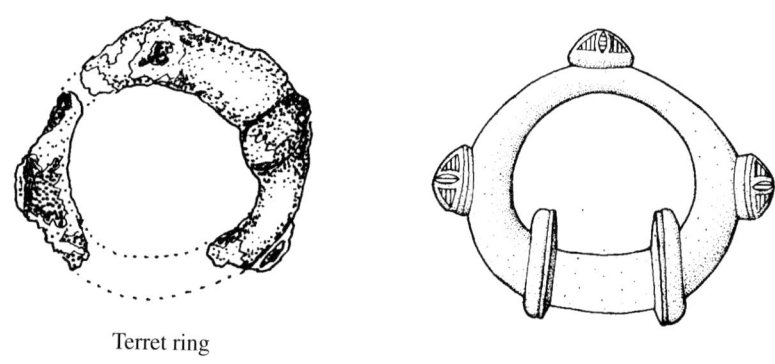

Terret ring

Above right is an example of a slightly later Iron Age terret ring shown complete.

Roman Pembrokeshire

The history of Roman occupation in Great Britain is quite well documented especially in parts of Wales like Caernarfon (Segontium) where a Roman fort was built around 78 AD and held around 1,000 men, down to Caerleon ("The Castle of the Legions" in Welsh) where 5,600 men were quartered.

But when you come to the history of south west Wales there is very little documentation about Roman activity. There are known settlements in Pembrokeshire like one at Amroth which may have been a lookout post with its views across the sea. Evidence has emerged in aerial photographs of a road from Carmarthen town towards the west coast of Pembrokeshire. As you can see from the following photographs and illustrations the Pembrokeshire Prospectors Society, through its finds has shown that the Roman influence is greater than previously believed. These artefacts and their findspots have been collated together by a local historian Mr John Roche of Pembroke who is producing a piece on Roman Pembrokeshire for the Pembrokeshire Historical Society's Journal. In addition the Pembrokeshire Prospectors record all their Roman finds with the National Museum of Wales. In this way the information we discover is made available locally and nationally to the widest possible audience.

Roman Enamelled Bronze Umbonate Disc Brooch 2nd Century AD

This brooch is called umbonate because it is shaped like an umbrella. Each of the small triangular cells was filled with coloured enamel. This was found in South Pembrokeshire. The enamel was blue, green and red.

Silver Denarius Septimus Severus 192 - 211AD

This coin forms part of another concentration of Roman finds from South Pembrokeshire. There is no sign of settlement nearby - the question arises ... why is there so much Roman material here if there is no settlement? Was it a trading station?

This kind of speculation is one of the pleasures of metal detecting. This particular coin was only recognised as such when its rim was seen in a hard lump of concretion around the coin. Careful and prolonged cleaning revealed a fine coin as seen above. Some of the concretion still adheres to the coin and is visible as the black marks on it.

Roman Trumpet Brooch 1st/2nd Century AD

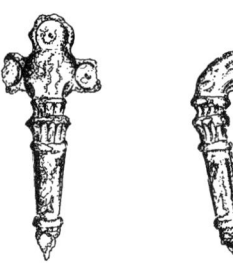

Roman artefacts of any sort are fairly rare finds in Pembrokeshire. This one was found near Pembroke and retains some enamelling on it stem.

Roman - British Trumpet Brooch with Headstud 1st - 2nd Century AD.

This brooch is part of the same group of finds as the silver denarius illustrated previously. Another theory concerning the location of their finding is that there may have been a vineyard there in Roman times. Who knows? One thing is certain, the Roman influence in Pembrokeshire is much greater than was ever thought and the Pembrokeshire Prospectors have helped to highlight this new knowledge with their finds of Roman objects.

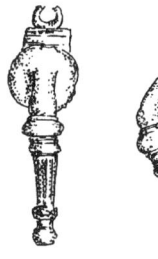

There have also been significant numbers of recoveries of Roman coins and artefacts in North Pembrokeshire. The essential thing about the Roman finds is that they are mostly coastal or near coastal. Far fewer items have come from inland Pembrokeshire. Perhaps this goes to support the view that the Romans were mostly only trading along the coast of Pembrokeshire and not maintaining any major inland presence? In which case, perhaps the Roman road into Pembrokeshire recently re-discovered might end at a river navigable down to the sea, one of the Cleddaus perhaps?

There is a legend quoted in Laws' History of Little England Beyond Wales (page 51) that Haverfordwest was originally Caer Alun and founded by Magnus Maximus or Macsen Wledig the former legionary who rose to the command of Wales and then sought to become the Emperor of all Rome's empire by usurpation. Haverfordwest does indeed lie at a favourite Roman building place. A ford crossing a river which was navigable to the sea. But there has been little evidence of Roman occupation ever found in or near Haverfordwest. Laws' again mentions (page 45) some Roman coins of the 3rd Century "dug up in the neighbourhood". The Pembrokeshire Prospectors have not found any Roman coins or artefacts in Haverfordwest as yet, but if we do we will have made a momentous discovery.

Here we have another Roman brooch, this time an oblong bow-brooch of the 2nd Century AD. This design is unusual and thought to originate from the continent. This was found in South Pembrokeshire.

Roman 2nd Century AD Oblong Bow Brooch

Another brooch again of a rare type is seen below. This is thought to be either a leech brooch or a boat brooch (so called because of its shape resembling a boat or leech). It appears to be unrecorded in Wales and indeed bears a strong resemblance to some Iron Age brooches. Further research awaits on this brooch.

Roman Leech or Boat
Type Brooch

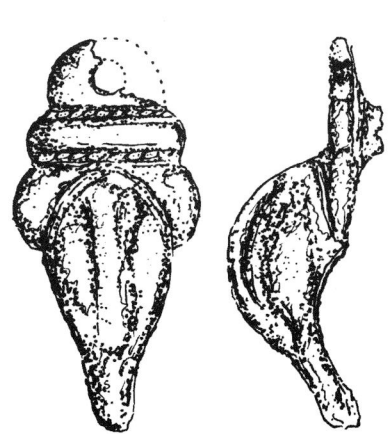

Another beach find and the detectorists first Roman coin. It was found at Amroth - which is where the previously mentioned Roman lookout? was situated. This coin is very worn but was very well struck and so enough detail survives to identify it. It has actually worn through in one part. The Pembrokeshire Prospectors feel they do an important service in finding items of history such as this coin which are otherwise going to rot away in the soil.

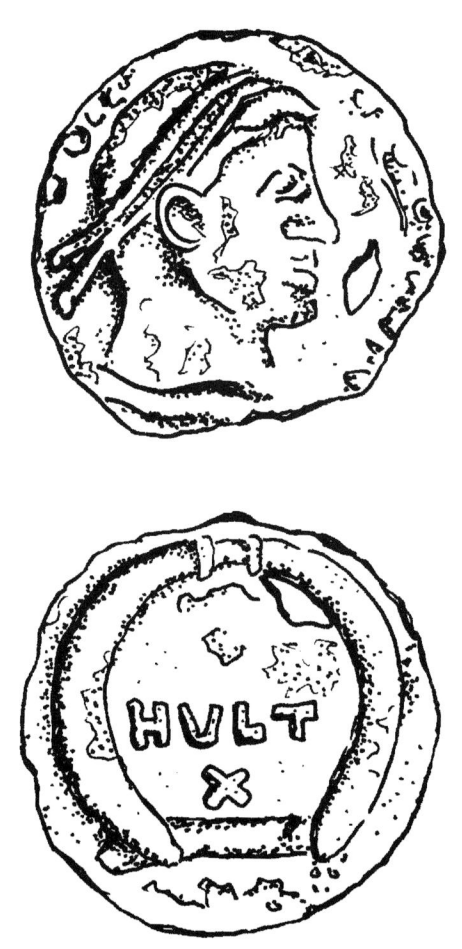

Silver siliqua of Julian II (Claudius Julianus) 360-363 AD.

Viking/Dark Age Pembrokeshire 400AD - 1100AD

Dark Age Pembrokeshire has apparently left little or no trace as far as the Pembrokeshire Prospectors finds record is concerned. Very little has been found in Pembrokeshire despite the other evidence of known occupation such as Viking place names, eg. Freystrop and the documentary evidence in the Welsh Records of St Davids and other places being attacked or destroyed by marauding Vikings. Those artefacts which have been found are, because of their rarity, all the more interesting and valuable in the context of Pembrokeshire's local history.

Gold Solidus of Justinian I
527AD - 565AD
Emperor of the Eastern Empire
Byzantine Era.

Gold Solidus of Phocas 602-610AD

These two coins were found at different times in the Tenby area and oddly enough by a father and son but not working together. Both coins are in such condition that one immediately thinks of their

Reverse of Coins Shown Above

having been protected - perhaps as part of a hoard? One has been pierced to be worn as jewellry perhaps? A very pleasant dream indeed-- a pot of very late Roman gold coins from the Eastern Empire waiting to be found somewhere in the vicinity of these two. Yes, the finders have been back and looked but without success YET! Another question arises! How did these coins come to be here? What trading network existed between Tenby and Constantinople where these coins were minted? Hours of pleasant speculation unfold when thinking about such things.

Moving on in time the next illustration shows a Bronze Viking Pennanular Brooch. This was found at Goodwick near Fishguard. The name Goodwick can be interpreted as Good Vick ie. Dark Age Scandinavian for Good Harbour which Goodwick certainly is. The flower design on each terminal can still be seen as can the remains of the red enamel which would have been present between the petals. This would have been used as a cloak fastener.

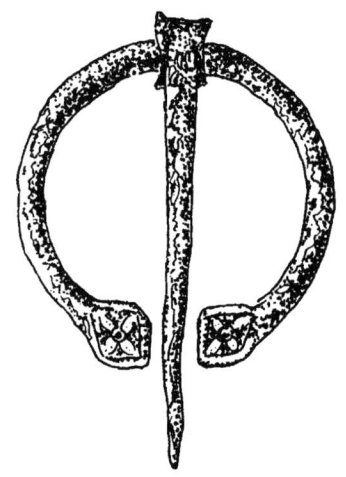

Bronze Viking Pennanular
Brooch 8th/9th century

Sword Pommel Viking Age
National Museum of Wales

A sword pommel fits onto the end of the handle and is usually rounded in order to not hurt the palm if the swordsman leans on his sword. It also helped to stop the sword flying out of the hand.

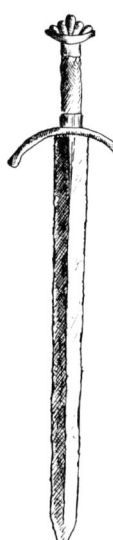

This sword pommel is of 9th or 10th century date. Similar examples have been found in Scandinavia, and one has recently been found on Anglesey. Swords resembling this have also been found in West Highland Scotland in graves dating to the 14th and 15th centuries.

The next find is a very rare one anywhere and doubly so in Wales. Only six coins of this type have been found in Wales. The Scandinavian connection in Pembrokeshire was mentioned earlier and this coin supports and amplifies the place name and documentary evidence. The Welsh of this time are generally reckoned not to have used coinage (indeed only one

"Welsh" coin of this period has ever been discovered - a silver penny of Hywel Dda who died 949AD - 950AD). Coins of this kind are a distinctly Saxon type and this particular coin was minted by Siigar who is thought to have been a moneyer in Derby. It is thought that Saxon coins of this age were generally brought into Wales by Viking raiders. This coin (or rather the fragments of it as can be seen in the illustration) was found at the Pembrokeshire coast near St Davids Cathedral which is recorded as having been sacked by the Vikings on a number of occasions.

Fragmentary 9th century Saxon coin

Because of its fragmentary state the coin cannot be certainly identified. Only three letters of the Kings name can be seen followed by REX (see illustration). However it seems likely that the King was either Eadred or Eadmund, both of whom reigned over the Norse Kingdom of York in the mid 10th Century AD. Eadred lost the Kingdom of York to Eric Bloodaxe!

One cannot help thinking when faced with a coin of this kind about the terror associated with the Viking raiders and one's mind swims with imaginings of burning thatched roofs, women and children screaming and running and men fighting desperately. Who lost this coin? A Welshman who had won it defending his patch or a Viking so loaded with booty he didn't notice or care about the loss of this one?

This coin was published in the British Numismatic Journal in 1985.

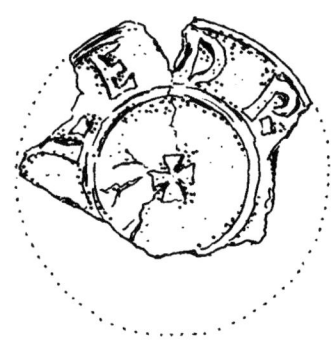

Medieval Pembrokeshire   1100AD- 1495AD

The Castles of Pembrokeshire are a lasting reminder of this period. Whereas the Welsh had generally dwelt in small scattered communities, the Normans built castles and established towns around these fortifications. In addition they enforced their own laws and customs and the domination of the Feudal Lordship. As the south of the county is the more fertile this was the land that the Normans seized and held onto. The native Welsh could have the poorer lands of the north. This situation led to a divide in the life of the county which is still existent to some extent today. Welsh is spoken more commonly in the north of Pembrokeshire and English placenames, etc, are more common in the south of Pembrokeshire.

The distribution of coinage finds from this time reflects the greater wealth in the south of Pembrokeshire at the time. We are much more likely to find a hammered coin or coins in the south of the county. Hammered coins were made by hand. A piece of silver roughly circular in shape was placed between two steel dies engraved with the designs of the coins two sides. When fitted together tightly the top one was struck sharply with a hammer and this impressed the engraved design of the die into the coin - thus a "hammered" coin. Some of these are found cut in half or quarters in order to make small change. Remember coinage was valued by weight of bullion in those days so a fragment of a coin still had some value.

Penny and Half Penny
Both London mint
Edward III (1327 - 1377)

Short Cross Penny
Henry II (1180 - 1189)
Found Mid. Pembrokeshire

Early Nuremberg Jetton 15th Century Found at Newgale

Jettons were originally designed as counters - literally for counting monies at the exchequer. Their name comes from the French "jeter" to throw, because they were moved at speed or even thrown across the counting board. There is some evidence that they may have had some use as small change also. The Tenby mathematician Dr Robert Rekorde wrote a book on mathematics in 1542 which devoted a lot of space to the use of these counters.

Slebech Hoard -Henry II 1154AD - 1189AD
Richard I 189AD - 1199AD

Early in December 1991, three members of Pembrokeshire Prospectors were detecting on a ploughed field in Slebech Park near Haverfordwest. One, Mr Arthur Duncan, found a hoard of twelve coins and the others did not. Luck plays a large part in this hobby and this example shows something of the attraction of our hobby. You never know what you will find, so keep digging!

The coins were scattered by the plough but eventually ten pennies and two cut half pennies were recovered. The Coroner was informed promptly and the coins were reported to the National Museum at Cardiff (standard practice for this society). Mr Edward Besly, Numismatist for the National Museum of Wales found that the coins were most likely deposited between 1195 - 1200 AD and that it was only the second hoard of short cross coinage recovered in Wales.

Below the collected coins, etc, of the Slebech Hoard

Picture from Besly: Welsh Hoards

Medieval Fair or Market Ground

One of the benefits that metal detecting has had is the tremendous increase in knowledge of local history as a result of the finds made and published by detectorists. Many detectorists visit road and building sites in order to search the disturbed ground. You never know what may be found, and so it was that in 1995, a new road was to be constructed into Haverfordwest. There was no expectation of finding anything other than some remains from an old dump which was known to be there. We obtained permission readily enough from the County Surveyor. Imagine our surprise and pleasure when hammered silver coins began to be recovered - so many infact, that we were hard pressed to keep up with the destructive activities of the JCB and bulldozer. Progress has to be made and therefore we recovered what we could but we cannot help wondering what was lost in the material taken away from the site and dumped.

Readers will note from the illustration that some of the coins have been cut. This was the practice of the day when a penny might be cut in half to make a halfpenny or quarters to make a farthing. This was because the purpose made smaller value coins were not available. Some artefacts were also recovered from the site including the lead seal seen on the next page.

The important thing about this now totally obliterated site was that it was unknown. The coins show activity for about five hundred years yet there is no mention of this site anywhere in Haverfordwest's archives. The fact that it is now known rests entirely on the efforts of the Pembrokeshire Prospectors Society.

This seal belonged to a lady named Alice It was found at the aforementioned site of an unknown fair or market ground which has now been totally removed to allow a new road to be built. The original is going to the National Museum of Wales at Cardiff and a copy rests with the Haverfordwest Museum. The design shows a vine or flowering plant which is surrounded by the lettering. Some of the lettering has decayed beyond deciphering but enough remains to see ALICE ___ERE. It is written in Lombardic capitals. Who was Alice? It seems unlikely we shall ever know.

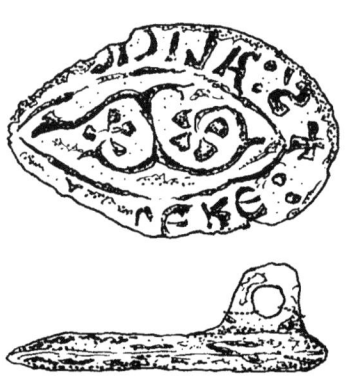

Lead seal matrix - middle to late 13th Century.

Pilgrims Ampulla 14/15th Century

This small lead object was the proof of someone's having made a pilgrimage to a shrine and returned. They were sold filled with holy water or oil. The ampulla was designed to be attached to clothing (see the attachment lugs intact on this ampulla). The flower motif is thought to refer to the speedwell, a flower which pilgrims put in their shoes in order to assure safe and speedy passage. Many of these objects are found far from any known shrine or route to a shrine. This is because they were often buried in farmland in the belief that this would ensure good crops. This basic design was common to many shrines and each shrine had its own special mark. The W of the Walsingham shrine in Norfolk is often found as is the scallop of Sant Iago de Compostela in Spain.

Papal Bulla : A lead seal of Pope John XXII 1316AD

This artefact would have been attached to a document or Bull issued by the Pope and was the proof of its authenticity. The design on the left-hand image shows two faces and a cross and the lettering SPASPE. This is a very shortened form of "St Peter and St Paul" in Latin and the design of the other side is a crudely lettered IOHNNES PAPA (or Pope) XXII. This translated from the Latin means John XXII (the twenty second) Pope. This design pattern was retained unchanged except for the names of the popes' for over 1000 years.

Pilgrims Lead Seal   Late 13th or Early 14th Century

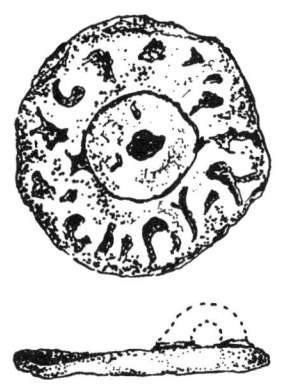

This object was found with an Edward Ist silver coin of 1305AD minted at Canterbury. The seal is engraved with Lombardic writing and the inscription reads "S'Keneric F'Resi" which means "Seal of Keneric, Son of Res". It was found near to a known pilgrim hospital in Pembrokeshire and may have belonged to a man on his way to St Davids. At this time two pilgrimages to St Davids were considered the equal of one to Rome and St Davids was consequently the busy destination of many pilgrims. Perhaps Keneric was one of them? The seal matrix will be on display at St Davids Cathedral.

Pilgrims Badge 14th/15th Century
Sew on type (note lugs)

Pilgrimage was a big industry in medieval times, many people required transport and lodging on their journey. Pilgrims required proof of their successful journey and this took the form of either an ampulla (see previous pages) or of a badge much as is illustrated here. No one really knows what the badge of St David's was, but it is thought that it would have been the Virgin and child. This badge shows such an image and is thought to be the first of its kind found in Pembrokeshire and is probably unique.

Another unique pilgrim's ampulla is shown below. At this stage, not much is known about it and it is being researched at the British Museum in London.

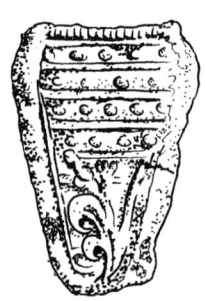

Medieval Bronze Strap-end Buckle. Mid 14th Century

This piece of a buckle probably helped hold together someone's cloak - it is only 3cms or so long and not very wide. It was rivetted onto a strap of leather which in turn was probably stitched to something else. Finds such as this were mass produced but probably not in Pembrokeshire. They are relatively common finds

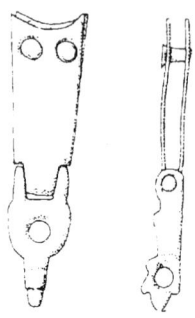

The next find is also a strap-end but was designed not as a fastener but to hold together and protect the material it was attached to. This strap-end is very small and may have been used to strap on a spur. Despite its small size it has been carefully designed and made. It carries enamelled designs on both sides and these designs are what makes this artefact so interesting.

The design as seen left, incorporates the three lions of England on the left and the arms of France viz the three Fleur de Lis on the right. At this time the King of England also controlled large parts of France and so the arms of England incorporated those of France. Whoever wore this buckle was showing that he had Royal connections by displaying these arms on his personal accoutrements.

The design on the other side of the buckle is as seen on the right here

and matches in all but one respect the arms of the de Bohun family. The difference is that the background colour in the arms (as known today) was blue but on the artifact it is red enamel. This is called in heraldic terms a change of tincture of the field. It is rare for this to happen but not unheard of. The de Bohuns certainly had Royal connections in that Humphrey de Bohun married (c. 1302) Elizabeth, daughter to John of Gaunt, grandaughter of King Edward III, a later de Bohun - Mary, married Henry IV (1399 - 1413).

This artifact was found in South Pembrokeshire and the de Bohun's had been Lords of Haverfordwest at about 1289 but afterward were mainly connected with Hereford. Despite this it does seem very likely that this artifact was the property of one of the de Bohun's. A metal detecting find is just the beginning of the process. Research leads into lots of strange fields and in this case we have been lucky in that we could call on the expert help of former Wales Herald Bard Mr Dillwyn Miles FSA.

Edward 1st penny

Coins of Edward I and Richard I

These two coins illustrate some of the features common to the designs of many medieval coins. The penny of Edward I is called a long cross coin because the coin had a cross on it which stretched over the complete diameter of the coin. This feature was supposed to stop the practice of "clipping" or trimming small slivers of silver off the coin without cutting into the portrait or the cross. Clip enough coins and you had a small ingot of silver It was punishable by having your hand chopped off however! The earlier coin of Richard I The Lionheart shows the

short cross which is contained within the small circle. These two terms have become commonly used as short hand for the type of coin, ie. "short cross" is before 1247AD and "long cross" after this date. The cross also acted as a guide for people to cut coins in half or even quarters as explained earlier (see page.18...).

Richard 1st penny

The coin illustrated is a cut half penny of Henry II 1154 - 1189 and is a short cross.

Lead Pilgrims Ampulla 15th Century

This ampulla follows the basic design of the one illustrated previously. It shows both arrow and shell motifs. The arrow represents either St Edmund or St Sebastian. Both were tied to trees and shot with arrows. These saints were popular during the 15th Century. Ampullae were the forerunner of our modern good luck charms.

Arrow   Shell

Adult Finger Ring 13th/14th Century

This ring was found on a beach in South Pembrokeshire. It is made of pewter which survives quite well in wet environments. The two protrusions imitate precious stone settings. They are in fact blank - ie. no space exists for a stone but they are cross hatched and this may have been to enable a coloured medium, perhaps enamel to adhere and thus imitate precious stones. In addition commoners were not allowed at this time to wear gold or silver jewellry In 1363 Edward III issued a decree forbidding Yeomen,Artisans,Wives or children from wearing jewellry made of gold or silver.This law remained in England until James 1st.Commoners were also forbidden to wear precious stones,pearls and belts or circlets of gold or silver.The law was not very well enforced but the maker

of this ring would seem to have been aware of the law.(Medieval Sumptuary Law). Pewter was known as poor man's silver because of its shine when polished.
Lead Tokens.

These are something of a puzzle. No one really knows what they were used for. They have been found to date from Medieval to Stuart times. It seems obvious that they were made to imitate coinage and perhaps were used as

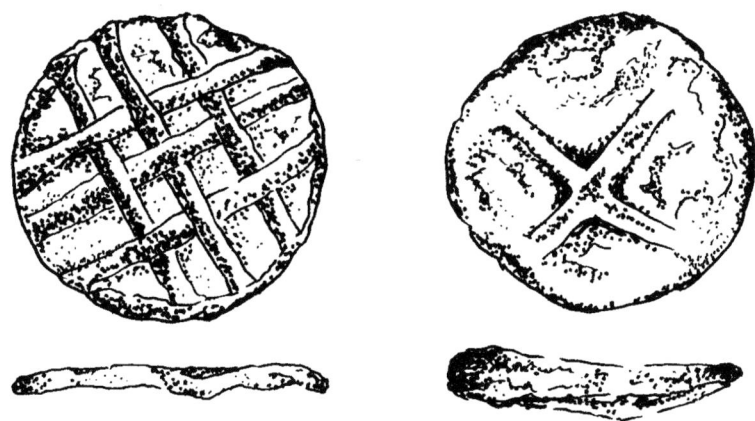

small denomination or value coins. They are found all over England and Wales. These were found on the shores of the Cleddau near crossing points. Perhaps they paid the ferryman!

Tudor Pembrokeshire 1485 - 1603AD

The accession of Pembroke born Henry Tudor as King Henry VII brought about the beginning of the end of the feudal system in the county. The Act of Union in 1536 led to Pembrokeshire as we know it and to English rule. This period also saw the introduction of machine made coinage "milled coins" which took over from hammered silver coinage. The coins of Elizabeth I are the most numerous coin finds made in Pembrokeshire. This could reflect the growing prosperity of Great Britain at the time.

Elizabethan Groat, Threepence, Half Groat and Penny

The above illustration shows some of Elizabeth I's coins which are a likely find in Pembrokeshire.

The next illustration demonstrates the increasing personal wealth in Pembrokeshire. Here is a gold ring set with twin rubies and with settings for four pearls which are sadly missing. Pearls being organic will rot in soil. This ring can be dated by its style to approximately 1600 - 1625.

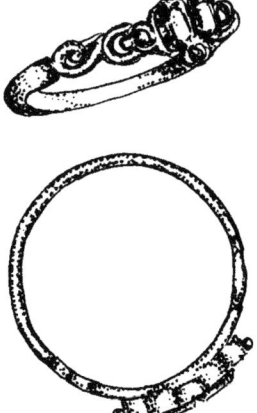

Ruby and Pearl Ring 1600 - 1625

Shown here are two coins of Henry VII 1485 - 1509. They are a groat and a penny respectively. The penny is interesting because it is a sovereign type. It shows the king seated on his throne and holding the regalia of Kingship, the mace in the right hand and the orb in the left.

Groat 1485 - 1509

Sovereign Type Penny 1485 - 1509 from the unknown fair or market site at Haverfordwest

This rampant lion is made from copper alloy. It was probably a harness mount and when new and in use it would have been polished brightly. It may have had heraldic significance to its owner - or it may have been designed for intimidation. "Don't pick on me, I'm as fierce as a lion" was the message. It dates to the 16th/17th Centuries. It was found along with the numerous coins from the unknown market or fair at Haverfordwest.

To own a horse in these days was to be a wealthy person. The poor were much poorer and the rich much more rich than in our times. As trade increased however, some of the poor developed into the Middle or Trading Class which is so numerous in our day. Another find which provides evidence of increasing personal wealth is in the following illustration. Although it is only a humble button it is made from bronze. It was cast and then decorated by hand with the design being punched out in individual dots. Poor people could not have afforded this. But it is not silver or gold which would have remained as the privilege of wealth to the few.

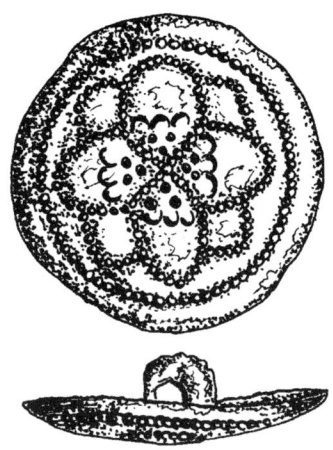

16th century Bronze Button Hand punched flower design

King Manuel I
Portuguese Gold Cruzado
1495 - 1521

This gold coin is in very fine condition as well as being a rare find for this country let alone county.Not surprising then that it won the newly instituted Gold Coin Cup,one of the Society's annual trophys.It was found near to the Bishop's Palace at Lamphey

This seal top silver spoon was found on a beach in South Pembrokeshire. A wet environment preserves silver very well and this spoon has survived its four hundred years in the sands admirably. This type of spoon was called a seal top because the flat top of the handle - known as the knop, was designed to have initials punched or engraved into it. As seen below a fictional example

This spoon would probably have been presented to a couple on the occasion of their marriage.

Although wealth was beginning to spread down through society, the more basic amenities of life were still far from common. Disease was still an everyday thing. Treatment might well have been a mixture of superstition and prayer. The next artefact demonstrates these beliefs quite well. It is a hollow sphere of bronze called a pomander, and it has an elaborate pattern of holes cut into it and engraved lines in parallel. It would have been worn on a chain around the neck and would have contained perfumed herbs and/or flowers. Its' purpose was to ward off infection or spells, ie. plague or witchcraft. This one dates to the 16th or 17th Centuries. Remember Haverfordwest had an outbreak of the plague in the late 17th Century which killed a large proportion of its inhabitants.

Bronze pomander 16th/17th century

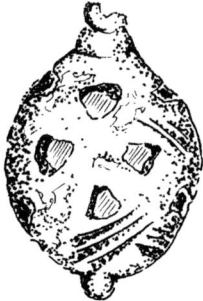

Gilt Bronze Pilgrim's Cross 16th/17th Century

Pembrokeshire's increasing wealth forms a backdrop to this time. Part of the reason for this wealth was the Pilgrim trade. People were still coming to St David's Cathedral in the belief that this still difficult and hazardous journey would help erase their sins.

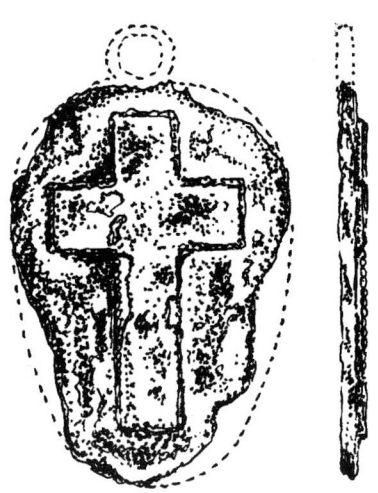

The ownership of horses as mentioned earlier, signified wealth. People were happy to show off their wealth in those days so everyday objects like horse harnesses were often richly decorated and here we have two examples.

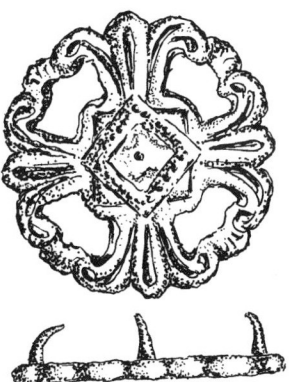 

Cast Bronze and Tinned Horse Harness Decoration Tudor Period
Lead and Bronze Plaque Heraldry Harness Decoration Bronze Shield set in a cast lead surround 16th/17th Century

These two decorations would both have been polished brightly and the right hand one could have had its owners initials engraved into the bronze shield. Rather like an expensive personalised number plate on your car today.

The next item although mass produced still has the charm and individuality of the hand made. The thimble is widely collected even in its modern form. The large numbers of early thimbles discovered in recent years by detectorists have greatly added to the popularity of thimble collecting.

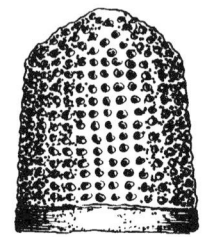

Tudor Beehive Thimble.

This Tudor thimble is cast bronze and was hand punched - sometimes the punches were done in a single continuous spiral line. Its' shape suggests its name - a beehive thimble.

The next items illustrated are equally common finds, perhaps even more common than thimbles. They are lead spindle whorls. They were used to weigh cloth ends down on a cloth weavers loom. Patterns of decoration like these have been found on spindle whorls datable from the 14th Century to the 17th Century. They are also found nationwide in Great Britain. Perhaps moulds were sold to itinerant merchants who made and sold these all over the country. More evidence of trade anyway.

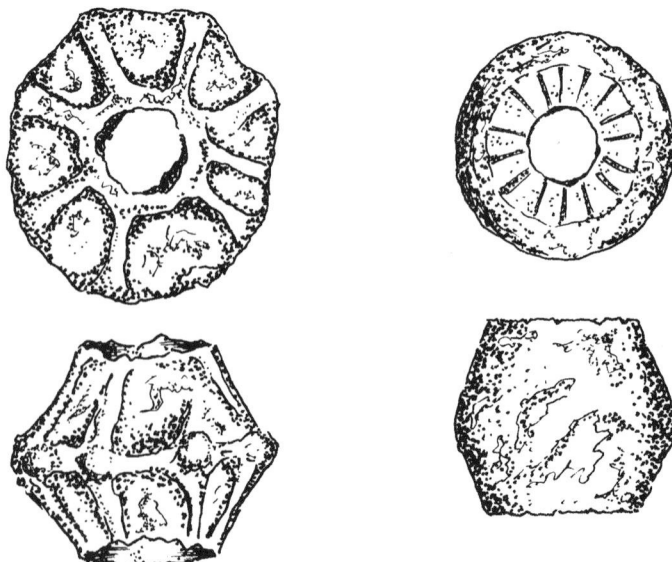

Lead Spindle Whorls

The following object, part of an official seal believed to be 16th century in date, was found in a field near Haverfordwest. The legend reads SIGILLUM AD RECOGNICONEM INFRA COMITATU which means Seal for recognition within the county. The other half of the seal would have had the name of the County to which the seal referred. It's round shape and size (Two inches in diameter) point to its use as an official seal. When found the seal still had green wax in it and it is known that green wax was made at this time by mixing verdigris into the wax. Most Town Councils will have in their possession a Town Seal, and in some cases this seal might be very old. Haverfordwest Town Council have just such a seal which is on display at the Town museum. The design on the seal found is as seen below.

Castle flanked by a lion and eagle 16th century town seal

This same design is found on the Common Seal of the Borough of Haverfordwest and is good reason for supposing that the part seal refers to Haverfordwest. See illustration below.

Stuart Pembrokeshire 1603 AD - 1714 AD

Pembrokeshire's rising prosperity has been mentioned in previous chapters. During this period Pembrokeshire was dealt two severe economic blows. The plague of 1651/2 severely damaged economic life in Pembrokeshire. One of its towns, Haverfordwest, lost more than one third of its citizens in this time. Before this happened the Civil War had done some damage in Pembrokeshire, most probably in terms of destruction, confiscation of property and lands by Parliament or the Crown and possibly also in looting by soldiers and by being forced to feed and water the invading or defending armies. Both the plague and the Civil War's left their marks in terms of metal detecting finds. During the time of the plague the dead were buried in special pits with quicklime. They often had a crude lead cross put in with

them and these have been found particularly near large medieval cities. So far none has turned up in Pembrokeshire. The Civil War left lots of relics however. Chief amongst this period's finds must be the Tregwynt Hoard. To quote its finder Mr Roy Lewis "The find of a lifetime". There had always been a legend of buried treasure at Tregwynt Manor in the North of Pembrokeshire. This had become confused with the Last Invasion of 1797 when some of the military people concerned were at a ball at Tregwynt on the evening of the invasion when news was brought to them. With this story in mind Roy had searched at Tregwynt but without much success. One day he was contacted by the owners of the Manor. They had done some soil moving in the grounds and would he like to search it? Always keen but without in this instance, much hope of finds, Roy came to search. After a while he found a hammered coin and very soon after another and another. He had soon found so many that it was obvious he'd found a hoard. He informed the owner and together they decided to hire a JCB in order to move the excavated earth and search more thoroughly. He also informed the National Museum of Wales and the Coroner. Eventually Roy found a total of 500 gold and silver coins, many of rare denominations and mints and nearly all in very fine condition. He later found a gold ring which added further to the mystery of the coins. The coins were found within the grounds of Tregwynt which belonged to the Harries family at the time of their burial. The Harries were Catholic and being a Catholic at the time of the Civil War was tantamount to being a Royalist. It was enough to merit your death possibly and certainly a great deal of "confiscation" of your property by the Parliamentarians. So it seems that somebody Harries of Tregwynt at this time may have buried his or her savings. The ring found nearby is a 17th Century gentleman's gold ring and engraved inside the band is the following inscription "Rather Death than Falce of Fayth". This motto indicates the wearer was probably not only a Catholic but also a Royalist- very dangerous in a time when just being Catholic was a reason for persecution. The fact of its being a man's ring would indicate the Mr Harries of the day, one Llewellyn Harries as being the one concerned but this can never be proven now. A Coroner's inquest held into the circumstances of the coin hoard and ring's burial and discovery, declared them Treasure Trove and they passed to the ownership of the Crown. They are all now being studied at the National Museum of Wales. The hoard has been recognised as Wales' "most important hoard of Civil War treasure" by the Museum. Truly the find of a lifetime.

James 1 Half Laurel
Gold Coin 1619-20

Charles I Declaration Half
Crown 1644.Oxford Mint

So named after Charles I "declaration" made at Wellington, Shropshire, September 1642,in which he promised to uphold the Protestant faith, the Laws of England and the liberty of Parliament.

The above is the best find from the Civil War period, but easily the commonest find is the lead musket ball shown left. Thousands of these have been found and continue to be found. They were either made in moulds or by dropping molten lead down a shot tower into water. They are often found in different sizes. Lead is a soft metal and would distort if it hit anything almost. When one finds such a flattened shot in the middle of a field one wonders whether it hit anyone rather than anything? Lead shot could obviously fly a long way from any battle ground and so a more certain indicator of a place where a skirmish took place would be the finding of a powder measure as seen below. A musketeer or soldier of the time had a powder horn and various other items hanging from a belt about his person. With these he would laboriously reload his musket and this may have taken a minute or so between shots. The muskets of the time were not accurate beyond short distances but they must have been dangerous in the right hands.

Lead powder measure

Some years earlier another hoard had been discovered in South Pembrokeshire. Not coin this time but pewter plate which had a direct connection to one of the main characters of the Civil War in Pembrokeshire.

Major General Rowland Laugharne

This portrait shows Major General Rowland Laugharne of St Brides, Pembrokeshire. This gentleman had fought for the Parliamentarians at first but then changed sides! This occurred in 1648 and it is no wonder that he had visits from Parliamentary officials who would have confiscated every valuable they could find. In 1649 Laugharne narrowly missed execution when he drew lots with Poyer and Powell, for one of them to be shot. Poyer was the unfortunate victim and he was shot in Covent Garden Piazza in London.

Laugharne claimed after that he had lost £37,650 during the war! A colossal sum when inflated to today's values. The plates which were found had been secreted in the bottom of an old pond not far from the drive to Laugharne's house. One was tucked inside the other two which were faced in upon each other. This explains the well preserved interior surfaces of the plates. Each plate is marked with the owners initials

L

R A

and this was done four times on the biggest plate or charger. One plate has a makers mark or stamp and initials IK either side of a tankard and the date 1624.

This date indicates end of the pewterer's apprenticeship, when he became a craftsman with his own mark. The plate must have been made within forty years of this time. The finder Mr Arthur Duncan is here seen with the pewter plates near the find spot
Picture copyright "Western Telegraph".

What exactly is this object? It is made from lead and variously described as a holy water font, a bird seed holder or a powder measure. Further research is being done and eventually we will know.

Lead what?

Buckles range from the utilitarian as seen below in the example of two bronze buckles of the 17th Century. But seen overleaf we have an extremely ornate bronze shoe buckle made to commemorate the accession of William and Mary in 1688.

Cast Bronze Buckles
Both these buckles are 17th century and were made to buckle on spurs.

Bronze Shoe Buckle 1688

Coins of the Stuart age are a mixture of hammered silver and milled silver. There were the usual copper coins also, but some coins were made with a tin plug in them. Seen right here we have a Charles I silver penny 1625 - 1649. This is reproduced life size.

Some larger denomination coins become more common finds in this period. This coin is a shilling of Charles I 1640 made at the Tower Mint in London

The next coin shows the reverse of a James I Irish shilling of 1605. The harp shows its Irish association

James I Irish Shilling

On the right we have the obverse of the Irish shilling showing the crowned Kings portrait.Found in a field in South Pembrokeshire. Nothing else was found with it to suggest why or how it came to be there.

James I Irish Shilling

Commonwealth half groat

This coin is a very poorly struck Commonwealth half groat or two penny piece. It was made by Parliamentarians and being as there was Civil War it was probably produced in a hurry hence the poor quality of the image.

The following coins although even more crudely made, have a very romantic past.

8 Reale piece,Philip IV of Spain

Minted in Mexico 1621 - 1665

These are the two sides of a piece of eight. The silver that these coins were made from was produced in Spanish controlled mines in Central and South

America. Before shipping back to Spain in a galleon it was hacked into roughly equal lumps and crudely struck with the images as seen above to show that it was silver and had passed through some sort of testing for purity, etc. This was found in a Pembrokeshire potatoe field which runs down to the shore. Is there a galleon out there slowly disgorging its' treasure or is this the casual loss of a sailor come back to his home in Pembrokeshire?

17th Century Posy Rings

be fayth full

Silver Posy Ring

A posy ring (so called because posy is a corruption of poesey - ie. short inscription) is one in which there is an inscription inside the band. Often this inscription is of a romantic nature. The rings were often given at betrothal but some rings were given under less committed circumstances also. The mottoes on these rings need no further explanation. The Pembrokeshire Prospectors are often called upon to find modern losses of rings and we know how much anguish the loss of a sentimentally valuable wedding or engagement ring causes to its loser. It must surely have been the same in the 17th Century.

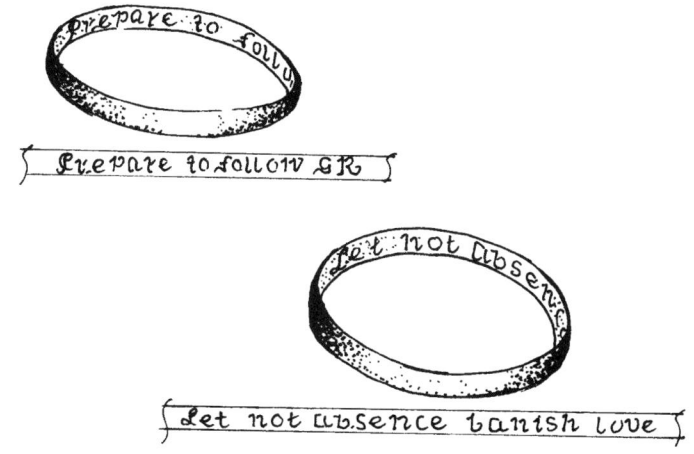

Prepare to follow GR

Let not absence banish love

Two Gold Rings

Towards the end of the 17th Century there was a nationwide shortage of small denomination coinage which meant life was difficult for shopkeepers and shoppers. There being no response to petitions from the citizens for something to be done people

Haverfordwest Copper Token Farthings, Undated but probably issued 1660 - 1670

took it upon themselves to issue coinage for local use. Thus it is that one finds farthing, half penny and penny tokens issued all over Great Britain during this time (1660 - 1670 in the main). They nearly all seem to have followed a basic pattern so perhaps there was some element of control from Government and the turning of a blind eye from the King whose prerogative it was to issue coinage.

The one illustrated previously was issued in two forms by T B Boulton of Haverfordwest. Mr Thomas Boulton, Gentleman has little known about him. He was evidently public spirited because being a gentleman he had no trade to follow and encourage with the issue of his own coin. Most tokens of this period were issued by Merchants who used the tokens both as coinage and to advertise their trade. Haverfordwest tokens are all very rare indeed and when this one was found (on a beach) the National Museum of Wales were very glad to receive it.

Man has always wished to show off his wealth and to embellish and beautify those things he valued most. Horses were still valuable and necessary to Stuart life and thus it is no surprise to find ornate items of harness decoration from this period. These items were probably mass produced and sold at fairs and markets. They were often made of brass which could take a bright polish. Some were made of lead which was tinned again to take a bright polish. Gilt examples have been found also. Horse brasses followed on from this tradition of beautifying your valued horse.

17th Century HorseHarness Decoration

We have seen in previous chapters how technology has developed through the ages and the metallic finds made have progressed from being hand made to the more recent machine made.

The next artefact shows how a problem was solved using the technology of the time. These things are called foot pattens and are the ancestor of the modern wellington boot. By standing on the wooden foot shaped platform and tying it to your foot you could walk on the iron ring bolted to the underside of the platform. This raised your foot up a few inches (9 or 10 centimetres) above whatever you walked on. Remember roads in towns often did double duty as rubbish dumps and sewers and must have been very unpleasant to walk on. Roads as we know them were a rarity in the country and in bad weather would soon have become muddy quagmires. It can be seen, therefore, that pattens were a necessary invention. There are records of their use from the 14th century to the middle of this century. The one illustrated dates to the late 17th century or early 18th century. At this time Birmingham had factories producing foot pattens, but it is likely that this one was made at a smithy nearby in Pembrokeshire.

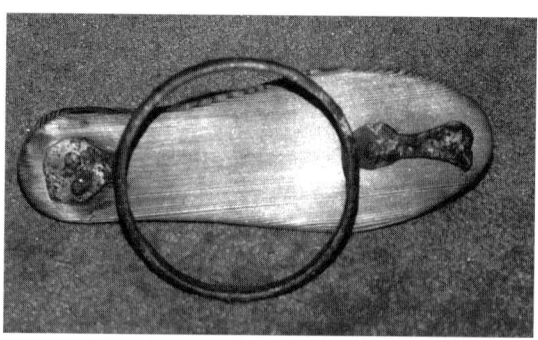

View from beneath: late 17th - early 18th
century foot patten

Pattens in use

Georgian Pembrokeshire 1714 - 1830 AD

The 18th century was a time of steady progress economically with trade increasing in the towns, and ports. Quays were built at remote creeks such as Abercastle, Porthgain and Solva to accommodate the extra trade. While this period saw larger scale mining of coal, History shows that despite economic progress , poverty abounds and Pembrokeshire was no exception, however a glimmer of hope came for some with an effort from public spirited people in education for the poor. Religion played an important role. Literacy came if at all, through the reading of the Bible. This period also includes The Last Invasion of Britain. The French landed an invasion force at Carreg Wastad near Fishguard 200 years ago .The Pembrokeshire Prospectors were invited to search the land at Carreg Wastad to look for relics of the French.Despite the presence of TV cameras to spur us on we were unsuccessful. But we do have plenty of other Georgiana to show!

Pembrokeshire, in common with most other parts of Great Britain saw a lot of rebuilding of houses and new houses being built for those whose trade prospered in Georgian times. Beginning therefore with trade we see the wool bale seals illustrated left. Pembrokeshire produced wool in large quantities from the Middle Ages on and each bale of wool was inspected and then sealed as passed by the Alnager, the official responsible for checking and guaranteeing the wool quality. These seals have date of 1752 and 1740? visible on them. It is not known to whom the initials on them refer, but further research may reveal this.

Trade is also represented by the next item, a crotal bell. These were attached to the harness of pack horses which were the main landbased method of transporting goods. This meant that you could hear a team of packhorses before you could see them and have plenty of time to get out of their way, because they didn't like to stop! These kinds of bell had a long period of usage from medieval through to Georgian times. More horse furniture is shown below.

Crotal Bell

Engraved Harness Boss, 18th century

This example shows the crest of Cawdor of Stackpole, one of the landed families of Pembrokeshire,and it would have been attached to the horse's harness

Other plainer bridle bosses of lead which would probably have been tinned or plated are shown here.

Again cast lead but showing a different style, these kinds of horse decoration have many different sizes and shapes limited only by the space on the horse's harness. This one perhaps, imitates a plume of feathers or a scalloped shell.

Scalloped Shell Harness Decoration

Apart from agriculture, Pembrokeshire's other main business was Maritime. This button can be reasonably accurately dated by means of the image on it which changed slowly over the years and also by the shape and method of attachment of the shank of the button on its reverse. This button dates to 1795.

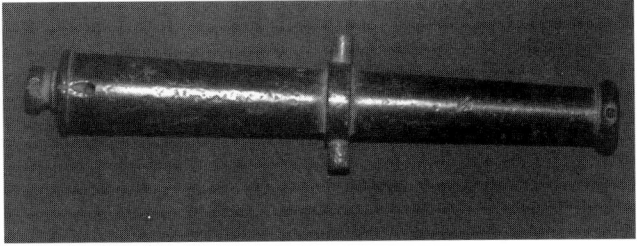

This replica of a cannon may be small but it is not a toy. It works and could certainly seriously injure if fired at you. This was not its purpose however. It's thought that this was a signal cannon used in conjunction with a lens and the rays of the sun to set off the cannon at a specific time of day - probably midday - when the sun's rays are at their strongest. Why would you want a miniature cannon report to signal 12 noon when there were perfectly good clocks to do the job? Probably it was used on an estate where the report could be heard at some distance and then all the workmen could break for lunch together. Perhaps it belonged to a retired naval officer who liked to relive memories of battle when he heard his signal cannon go off!?

There are no sign posts on the sea and accurate navigation depended upon accurate measurement as well as experience and knowledge.

These brass dividers - brass so as not to interfere with the compass - helped measure distances accurately. They were found on a beach in South Pembrokeshire.

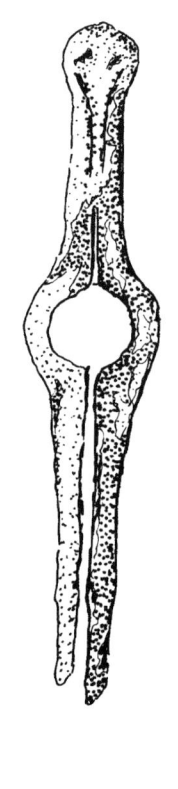

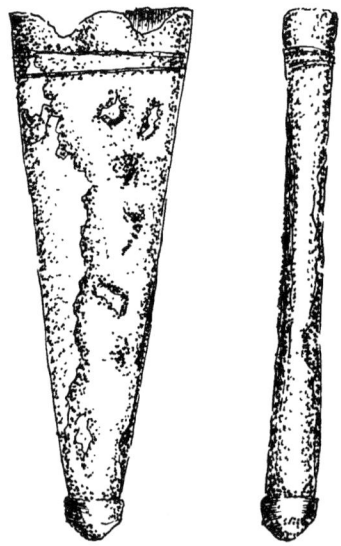

Dagger Chape

This little item formed the bottom end of a dagger scabbard and helped to secure the material of the scabbard together as well as decorate it. Being made of bronze it would polish well. The style is again one which had a long use. Examples like this can date from the 15th century to the 18th. A much more precise date can be made for the next item which is a silver shoe buckle. The Georgians were just as subject to fashion as the people of today and fashions for buckles as well as clothes changed quite rapidly in Georgian times.

This one can be dated to 1780 - 90 and would have looked very fine. As well as brightly polished shoe buckles a person would also have worn other items of polished metal about them.

These next items are buttons but not nearly so prosaic as our workaday modern buttons. They were nearly always made of copper, bronze or pewter and then tinned, silvered or gilt in order to make a brighter shine. They were made to be worn in sets so the general effect of eight or so buttons would have been very showy.

Decorative copper button   Ornate starburst button   Ornate button some gilding

Buttons of this kind are common detecting finds but do not always come up in good condition owing to soil conditions etc., enough are found for them to be a popular collecting field with some people.

Another everyday item which has become a popular collecting field is the thimble. Illustrated is a brass machine patterned adult size thimble. Because of their popularity a lot of research has been done on them and thus we can date this one to 1750-1800.

Georgian brass thimble

Georgian silver thimble

The thimble illustrated left here is especially collectable as it is silver and has engraved initials of its owner upon it between a device of two birds. Thimbles like this were made in large numbers with the space left blank for a local engraver to cut the initials or sometimes a motto. There is a hallmark of a letter B in an oval but so far this remains unidentified, however the thimble can be dated to 1700-1750.

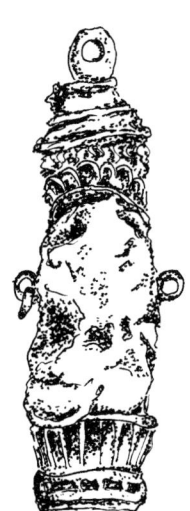

These two views show a silver bottle 2 x life-size in the form of a lion or dog. It has suffered quite a battering from the plough and is thus hard to identify exactly. The hallmark is legible and shows it to be from Birmingham and dates to 1797. It's purpose was to contain smelling salts or some perfume. Remember mains sewers had not yet been invented so there were powerful smells about to which this bottle had the remedy.

This item of Georgian material actually shows one of the Georges, the Fourth to be exact. It is in a gold guinea of 1822 which was found in the sandunes at a popular Pembrokeshire beach. Who knows what frolics led to its loss in the first place? Gold being heavy moves down rapidly in soft sand and so it was not until the great storms of 1987 moved quantities of the sand away that this coin was found. It has not been tossed about by the waves and so its condition is relatively good with only slight wear on the surface. Gold coins of any age are rare finds and this coin was that years winner of the Prospectors annual gold coin cup.

More Georgian coins, but this time silver. They are relatively common finds and usually in better condition than the copper coins of the same period which do not often survive well in Pembrokeshire's soils.

To get an idea of the size of these leg irons you should imagine the cuff around someone's ankles. They would have restricted your stride greatly. You could barely shuffle along when wearing these and the cuffs must have chafed horribly. They date from the 18th century and, amazingly, can still be locked and unlocked. Prisoners of the 18th century, especially the more dangerous felons would have been forced to wear these. They might also have been used on slaves (the slave trade was still being pursued at this time). They were found after a storm on a South Pembrokeshire beach and it is thought that they had washed in from deeper waters.

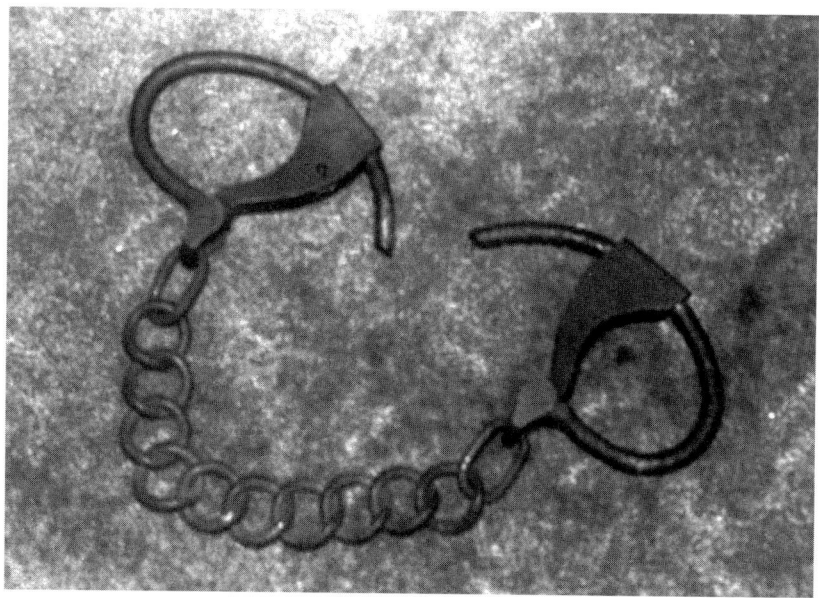

Victorian to Modern Pembrokeshire

The coming of the railway improved the economic life of the county but was the death knell for the extensive maritime industry. Goods and people would henceforth tend to be moved via the trains and not via sail. On the other hand agriculture was suffering a slump. Prices were low and rents high. Protest riots were common. These achieved a focus in the Rebecca Riots of 1839 - 1840's. Despite this widespread poverty people in general still had more in the way of material goods. Consequently Victorian finds are quite common.

Coin finds of this era are so plentiful, especially the copper and silver examples, that lack of space precludes their inclusion. Gold coins though are rare finds.

 Queen Victoria Gold Half Sovereign Young Bunhead Portrait 1853. Found in South Pembrokeshire.

Victorian Bunhead Sovereign

Reverse of Sovereign

Another gold artefact is the ring seen below.

This ring is fashioned from 18 carat gold and is made in the shape of a buckle.

Silver artefacts of this period generally turn up in excellent condition as the following examples show.

Mid Victorian Ring

This brooch was made in Birmingham to celebrate Queen Victoria's Silver Jubilee 1837 - 1887. It was found in what is now a potato field in South Pembrokeshire.

Victoria Jubilee Brooch

The Victorians were very melodramatic about death. Mourning was a very serious business and you had to have proper mourning clothes and jewellry. Jet was a favourite material for such items because of its colour black. The next item is a silver mourning brooch. Originally it probably contained a lock of hair from the deceased. We do not know the significance (if any) of the scene displayed on it. Perhaps a reader can enlighten us?

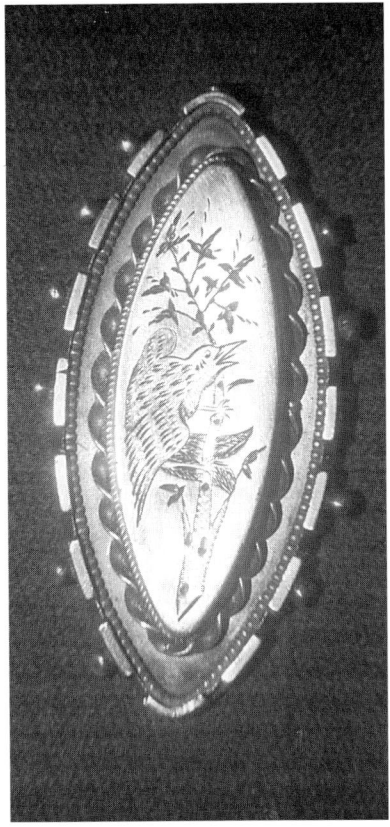

Silver Victorian Mourning brooch   Hunting Brush

The next item is a little more jolly. Again made of silver this is the back of a gentleman's brush. It depicts various hunting scenes of dogs chasing stags and boars.

During the First and Second World Wars there were many field camps in this area for Allied Forces on training exercises, etc. There were also prisoner of war camps in Pembrokeshire as well. It is not surprising then that many cap badges and regimental buttons found their way into the soil as well as ammunition, etc. The Royal corps of Signals cap badge seen below has the motto Quo Fas Et Gloria Ducunt (Whither Duty and Glory Lead). Both badges were recovered in Mid Pembrokeshire. From the same field comes a poignant reminder of our American Allies. A silver name tag in the form of a bracelet engraved on one side R C KNEESKERN 32589074 and on the other side LOVE SHIRLEY 12.25.43 (25th December 1943)

Cap Badge - Royal Regiment of Artillery

Cap Badge - Royal Corps.
of Signals

We have tried in vain to return this to its owner or his descendants. Perhaps it was a Wartime romance best forgotten now. Perhaps it's owner died in the war. Who knows? If any reader can help further with this puzzle we will be grateful.

During the 19th or early 20th Centuries families of substance would have had their coachmen and other servants dressed in smart livery (a kind of uniform) complete with the family's crest depicted on their buttons. The buttons would usually have been gold gilt or silver plated. These buttons are often found and their locations give fascinating insights into the movements of the families and of their servants. Some areas have been known to contain up to four different families' buttons. Most notable have been fields alongside old churches where the coachmen waited, tending the horses, etc. while their employers attended religious gatherings. Groups of these livery buttons are also found alongside old woodlands, possibly indicating some meeting point prior to the hunt?

This button belonged to the Mirehouse family of Angle and Brown Slade.	Leach family of Corston

Arm in Armour Holding Sword

Swan on a Bugle

Mathias family of
Haverfordwest

Boy with Snake about Neck

Upper half of Bull
surrounded by motto in
Welsh.

Philips family of Picton
(Lord Milford).

Lion rampant, collared
and chained
with Coronet above

James family of Pontsason,
Moylegrove. The motto which is in
Welsh reads Ffyddlon At Y
Gorphen. This means either
Faithful to the End or Faithful at the
End. Most likely the former. It is
rare to find Welsh upon any artefact
so this button is all the more
interesting for that.

Sir Charles Philips of Picton (formerly Charles
Fisher), to fulfil conditions of a marriage
settlement, had to change his surname to Philips.
This family crest makes a visual pun on this
change of name and its' circumstances.

Lion rampant collared
and chained alongside
Kingfisher before
Bullrush, holding Fleur
de Lys

Morgan family of Carmarthen.
This family had connections
with St Davids.

Stags head with antlers

Lord Cawdor of Stackpole

Baron de Rutzen of
Slebech Park

Swan with Coronet

Boar with Coronet
above and below

These are just a few of the livery buttons we have discovered. Some have not yet been identified. This is another of the pleasures of metal detecting. When you cannot go out to find relics you can get out your reference books and start finding out more about the objects you have found. In this way, metal detectorists become experts in many obscure fields of learning such as Military Cap Badges, Ammunition, Heraldry, Horse Furniture. Today after twenty or so years of metal detecting many detectorists are committing their knowledge to paper and making it available to all. Some of these books are the recognised reference works used in Museums, etc. An example of this would be Richard Hattatt's three volumes on Iron Age and Roman Brooches.

Horses were until the Second World War still an important part of agricultural life. Nowadays they are only a leisure pursuit. These brass makers plates would probably have fitted onto the horses nose band and showed who the harness was made by. They are essentially an advertising medium but were probably polished up along with all the other brass horse furniture for shows and other high days and holidays.

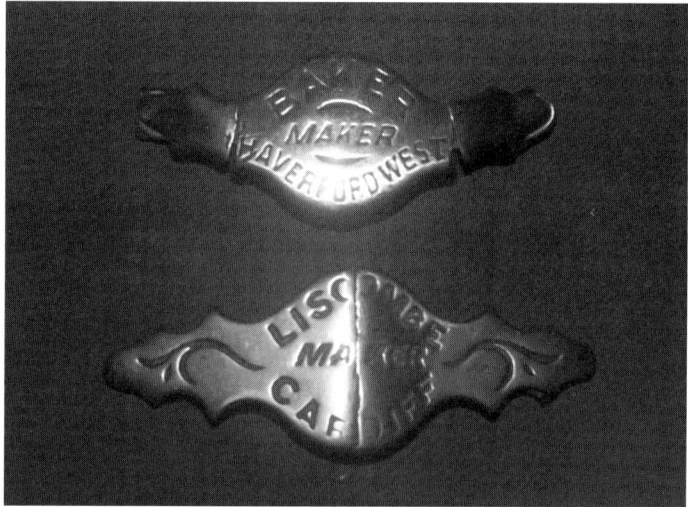

Horse Harness makers advertising brasses 19th or early 20th Century

One often comes across small concentrations of these finds in fields. This was explained by one old gentleman who recalled how when the tractors first came to his farm and proved their worth "Well, the horses had to go didn't they. No work for 'em anymore and once they'd gone, well all the tack was carried out into that field there and burnt. It smelled to high heaven, I remember that". Oral history in the telling.

Another common find which is also an advertisement is the trouser or fly button. In the time of ubiquitous zips it's hard to imagine how things must have been when you only had buttons to rely on.

The names on the buttons would have been advertising the shop or tailor's at which you purchased the clothes. Buttons from outside Pembrokeshire are quite common and one from Welshpool is illustrated here. These buttons obviously contribute to local mercantile history and form a jump off point to research and discover who the people advertised were.

Pressed metal trouser buttons

More buttons, this time examples of uniform buttons. Many work forces were issued with work uniforms during the late 19th and early 20th Century years. The one below left was worn by an employee of the Pembroke Dockyard Company.

The button below right belongs to a militia called the Royal Pembroke. Again more research is called for to establish exactly who they were.

Pembroke Dockyard button

Royal Pembroke button

A change from buttons now. How did this spoon end up in the middle of a field? Was it a picnic? Was it dropped on a journey? Whatever, it survived its burial well and must have been a pleasant surprise to its finder.

Yet more buttons. These are copper alloy and are called Hunting Buttons for obvious reasons. Both show what look like foxes - the first has a duck in its jaws. These would have been worn by the Master of the Hunt and his assistants. They might also have been worn by members of the particular Hunt.

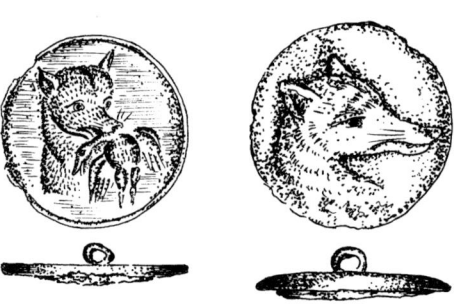

Victorian Silver Mustard
Spoon. Hallmarked 1888

Cast copper alloy one piece Hunting Buttons.

As technology advanced and mass production made goods cheaper, buttons proliferated and became more specialised. We have already seen livery buttons and advertising buttons. Here we see an example of what are called sporting buttons.

To the cricketing enthusiast this button will be fascinating. Look at the bails, how wide they are compared to today. The cricketer himself is obviously prepared to work hard as his sleeves are rolled up and he stands in short britches. Notice also the lack of pads or protective gloves. Our forefathers were obviously made of sterner stuff!

19th Century Cricketing button

More buttons follow: This one is a silver faced button of circa. 1840. This button was made in three pieces, the face, the back and the shank. The method of construction, the shape of the shank are all clues which can help to date such buttons quite precisely. This is a help because it gives a defined period of when the design on its front was in use. The family crest shown has not yet been identified but the crown above the shield indicates that the bearer of the arms was ennobled.

Silver faced Coachman's button
circa. 1840

The next button is plainer but only just. It is a cast one piece button of pewter and has an engraved design of initials upon it. We have no idea of who B G was and there is little clue from the button as to where to begin looking.

Engraved pewter one piece
button

The hobby of metal detecting turns up many interesting items. Often what is retrieved has some personal connection as in the seals of the Mediaeval times or the posy rings of Tudor times. In this case we have love tokens made for named persons. The practice of making love tokens from coins seems to have started in the Middle Ages when a young man would demonstrate his ardour (and his strength!) by bending a silver coin first one way and then the other. In this way the coin would become 'S' shaped when looked at side on.

In Victorian times a young man used not his strength but skill to show his love. The illustration shows a shilling of George IV (on the left) and one of Edward VII (on the right) both lovingly engraved. Obviously the face value of the coin was outweighed by the sentimental value created by their engraving in this way. They were keepsakes, not for spending. Whose mother was it for and who was Nellie? That is what we would like to know.

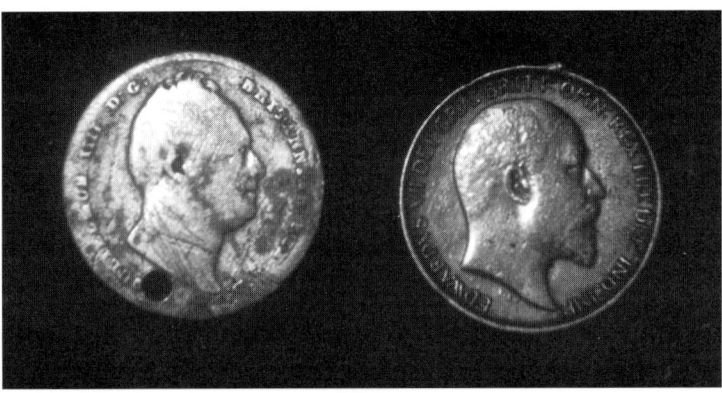

NOTES